THE

Leadership Innovation Manifesto

DR. KIM HIRES

13TH & JOAN

For permission requests, write to the publisher, addressed "Attention: Permissions Coordinator," 205 N. Michigan Avenue, Suite #810, Chicago, IL 60601. 13th & Joan books may be purchased for educational, business or sales promotional use. For information, please email the Sales Department at sales@13thandjoan.com.

Printed in the U. S. A.

First Printing, November 2019.

Library of Congress Cataloging-in-Publication Data has been applied for.

ISBN: 978-1-953156-22-8

DEDICATION

I dedicate this book to:
My fearless life partner, Kyle
My heartbeat, Blake
and Leaders who have the courage to run towards change.

ABOUT THIS BOOK

THE LEADERSHIP INNOVATION MANIFESTO was written with the busy Leader in mind. It can be read cover to cover just like any other book, and should take the average reader about three hours to complete.

For those who wish to use this book as a guided study for individual or team development, it is recommended to review one declaration per session. For maximum impact, sessions should be held at least once a week.

Session 1: *Let's Talk About Meaning; The Value of Innovation; Innovation is My Legacy*

Session 2: *Couponing is Not Innovation*

Session 3: *Imagination > Memory*

Session 4: *Leaders are Not Lion Tamers*

Session 5: *Leadership Capacity Determines Innovation Capacity*

Session 6: *Leadership Evolution Will Set the Pace for Innovation*

Session 7: *Innovation Requires Community; Innovation and Leadership; Conclusion*

Let's go!

TABLE OF CONTENTS

PREFACE

W HEN WE CHANGED how information was exchanged from human to human, the demand for innovation increased exponentially. Organizations' obsession with controlling how the organization is seen by the consumer shifted from a quarterly challenge to an hourly challenge. Today's consumer wants products and experiences that are better and different. How does a Leader establish the organization as better and different? The answer is *Innovation*.

However, when you get most Leaders behind closed doors, away from the public relations department, prying ears and smartphones, you find that most Leaders hate innovation. Yes, *hate*. Why? Because although innovation can lead to change, it starts off as an expensive experiment.

There are many models about how to implement innovation. The problem with implementation models is that creators of the models assume people *want* innovation. Innovation is a fancy word for change. The basic premise of this book is: *Innovation can only be successfully implemented and sustained when we change leadership and workforce mindsets about change.* Everything starts with a thought. A thought becomes a belief. Beliefs dictate actions. Culture is a collection of actions guided by beliefs. Therefore, a culture of innovation starts with leaders' beliefs about change.

In my industry, we rely on case studies to help students comprehend and apply important concepts. This approach allows students to see real world examples and make decisions with minimal risk. That's what I want you to do. I looked back at my personal experiences in higher education and coaching. I also combed through research and historical moments. In most of the cases, the outcomes speak for themselves. However, I don't want you to read about a case then walk away. Application is a crucial part of learning with case studies. After you read each chapter, take the time to answer the questions. The questions cause your brain to make connections between concepts and what you see in your organization, so when you encounter similar situations they will feel more familiar and less foreign. Your brain will not have to start from scratch and the situation will feel less threatening.

I wrote this book for Leaders at all levels: emerging Leaders, mid-level Leaders and senior executives. Your team mirrors your example. If you groan at the thought of change, then the team will groan at the mention of innovation. I coach Leaders to develop the mindset and skills to embrace change in their organizations and their lives. My system works from the inside out. Most models for innovation work primarily with external factors or from the outside in. My system helps Leaders shift their mindsets, get unstuck, and create fertile environments for innovation.

I'm in this with you!

Dr. Kim

The ability to read
and the ability to
comprehend
are two different
skill sets.

INTRODUCTION:
LET'S TALK ABOUT MEANING

MY DISSERTATION CHAIR was a woman of Chilean and Italian descent. She had incredible energy, a nurturing kindness and a strong accent. Sometimes understanding English was a bit of a challenge for her, but it was a help to me because without a bit of a language barrier, I would not have been able to keep up with her. It was as if the language barrier forced her to slow down. Her brain fired non-stop. The woman was (and still is) simply brilliant. Her research productivity is inspiring. She is a true expert in her field and a genuinely happy person, a rarity in academia.

Because of her challenges with English, she had a habit of asking the meaning of words. During our meetings she would ask, *Keeem [Kim], What this mean?* As I wrote my dissertation, of course I didn't appreciate being asked to constantly define my concepts. It wasn't until I had my own doctoral students to guide that I began to understand why she insisted that I define every concept. Not only is it a part of the scientific process as it ensures appropriate measurement of phenomena, but it also allowed her to see if I understood what I was doing and ensure we were on the same page. While it took me two solid years before I even looked at my dissertation again after graduation, defining concepts is still a frequent practice of mine.

Meaning

It is not until you can define a word that you can truly think about the word and demonstrate a good understanding of it. Here are key words I want you to think about as you read this book.

1. Leadership
2. Innovation
3. Manifesto

Let's look at each of them.

As of the writing of this book, a Google search for **leadership** produces 1,010,000,000 results. The definition of leadership that I prefer is *the ability to influence the character, development, or voluntary behavior of someone.* Yes, the *voluntary* behavior of another person. It's not *how do I make someone do x.* Humans must first understand what it is that you want them to do, then see the value in taking action *before* they act.

Next, let's look at **innovation.** Such a sexy word, but often terribly misused. A Google search for innovation yields

824,000,000 results. I hate to burst your bubble, but it's not a 21st century word. It actually dates back to the Middle Ages and first appears around 1540. Innovation comes from the Latin words *innovare* and *innovatus*. The direct translation means to renew (begin again) or change (to make different). So the definition of innovation that I will use for this book is *to make an existing thing different*.

The last word is **manifesto**. A Google search produces 80,900,000 results. You don't hear this word used often. The infrequent use may be due to the negative connotation associated with the way it has been used with certain types of government regimes and political parties, but like most words, it's harmless when you truly know what it means. All political parties and governments have a manifesto. We're familiar with the concept of *manifesto* by other terms: declaration, proclamation, policy statement, platform. The intonation of *manifesto* sounds like I'm saying it with bravado. And I am.

According to Merriam-Webster's Dictionary, manifesto means *a written statement declaring publicly the intentions, motives, or views of its issuer*. Like *innovation*, *manifesto* has Latin roots, but pre-dates *innovation*. We see *manifesto* appear in the 14th century. It is a combination of the Latin words *manifestus* (obvious) and *manifesto* (make public). The direct translation is making something readily perceived by the senses. In this book, I am communicating foundational beliefs about innovation that every Leader needs to have to create a culture in which employees run towards change instead of running away from change.

Let's look at all three key words again:

1. *Leadership*—the ability to influence the character, development, or voluntary behavior of someone.
2. *Innovation*—to make an existing thing different.
3. *Manifesto*—a written statement declaring publicly the intentions, motives, or views of its issuer.

Why don't I know this?

You may be thinking, *I thought I knew what those words meant, as they are used often enough,* but how many of us use words that we may not fully comprehend?

My intent with this book is to share my motives for innovation within the context of leadership. My thoughts in this book are shaped by my experiences, observations and conversations with clients, colleagues and students. I am a Leadership Coach. The essence of coaching is the ability to understand you: to think how you think and understand your perspective. I do this by asking questions, never telling you what to do (that would be consulting). The questions help to create a framework of your thought patterns for me. From this framework, I fit another perspective on top of yours—stretching and growing you to expand to the new framework. Done right, coaching identifies your blind spots and demolishes limiting mindsets. Quality coaching paves the way for you to perform at your maximum potential and to bring forth the best version of you. The best version of you is usually stuck in an outdated framework or a framework that will not support the next version of you.

I have worked with enough people in my career to know how the average leader thinks. I'm willing to bet my son's college fund that we did not think of the same definition for any of the key words. Why? Because we were not taught to. You may have thought *leadership* meant someone who guides people to complete a task, confused *innovation* with invention, and believed that *manifestos* were only used with communist and socialist ideals. Knowing the definition is half the battle. Education alone does not equip leaders because we don't lead primarily from what we know, we lead from the essence of who we are and what we believe.

With this book, I am placing a new perspective on top of your perspective. Behavior change starts in the mind. I must give you words and assign new meaning to them. In this book, I present new mindsets about leadership and innovation with my manifesto. This method works. How do I know? It's the foundation of coaching and behavior change.

But before I introduce the new paradigm, let's look at the value of innovation.

Mindset Shift Questions:

1. Prior to reading this chapter, what were your definitions of *leadership, innovation,* and *manifesto?* Write them below.

Leadership

_____

_____

_____

Innovation

_____

_____

_____

Manifesto

_____

_____

_____

2. How do your definitions differ from the definitions presented in this book?

_____

_____

_____

Innovation is the
only way to create
value by raising
capital and labor.

THE VALUE OF INNOVATION

IN MAY 2019, the results of the highly anticipated annual CEO and Senior Business Executive Survey from Gartner was released. Gartner is the world's leading research and advisory company and a member of the S&P 500. For this survey, data was collected in the fourth quarter of 2018 from 473 CEOs of organizations with annual revenues of at least $50 million. 60% of participants led organizations with $1 billion or more in annual revenue.

53% of the CEOs identified growth as a top priority. 21% identified their workforce as a top priority. Only 8% viewed innovation as a top priority. If you didn't scratch your head with those stats, you should. Something seemed off, right? According to the survey, CEOs rank growth above workforce and innovation. The logical priority ranking should be workforce, innovation, then growth. I'm not surprised by this priority list. It's important to note that the number of CEOs who identified growth as a priority increased from 40% in 2018 to 53% in 2019. Why? Because most CEOs assume growth is the most important indicator of success for a business.

In all fairness to them, they can't help it. A fair amount of CEOs started their careers in production, marketing or sales. Selling products or services is their comfort zone, and that's why growth is the favored indicator of success. A very rudimentary explanation of the logic is if we are growing, then we are selling. And there's absolutely nothing wrong with that logic except for the fact that products and services offer limited value. When leadership holds on to that mindset, they become enslaved to supply and demand. The organization exists at the mercy of the market.

So how do organizations get freedom? Innovation. As Forbes contributor Greg Satell explains, innovation raises the productivity of the capital and labor. Innovation frees organizations from supply and demand by creating entirely different markets. Every industry can benefit from innovation. Big businesses, universities, governments, even small businesses and cities can benefit from innovation. We can even benefit from embracing innovation in our personal lives. Why can't we benefit from leveraging our time and talents in unique ways?

Pathway to Innovation

Innovation is not a one and done process. It's a never ending process of discovery, creation, revolution and evolution.

It changes everyone involved in the process. If that's not an approach Leaders are comfortable with, then we can begin to understand why only 8% of CEOs identified innovation as a priority. When a Leader's career starts in production, marketing and sales—all of which measure time and tasks with firm endings, innovation can seem like a bottomless pit where resources disappear. As a Coach, this is also a sign that Leaders struggle with personal innovation too. Resistance to innovation often aligns with an innate resistance to change. More on this later...

Harvard Business Review published an article on the challenges of innovation. Within the context of leadership, most Leaders do not know how to define innovation. See, there *is* power in truly defining things! If you can't clearly define your problem, you will spend thousands of dollars and ridiculous amounts of time only to waste even more time. The right solution starts with identifying the right problem. For Leaders, the problem is never making more money. Create the right product or service and you WILL make money. So, what type of innovation is the best fit for your organization?

Types of Innovation

According to Satell, there are four types of innovation: Basic Research, Breakthrough Innovation, Sustaining Innovation and Disruptive Innovation.

Basic Research (BR) is the first type of innovation. With this type of innovation, the problem is not clearly defined and Leaders have one goal: to discover something new. BR requires high capital and highly skilled labor. It is not unusual for organizations to partner with academic institutions to tap into existing cultures of research for this type of innovation.

The next type of innovation is called Breakthrough Innovation (BI). With BI, the problem is clearly defined and different entities work simultaneously on solving the problem. Most breakthroughs of the 20th century were developed this way. The COVID -19 vaccine was created using this type of innovation. Organizations may work with other organizations in different geographical locations, sectors or industries. The level of involvement of each organization is determined by the expertise available within the organization and how the innovation will benefit the organization and whether the innovation can be sustained.

Sustaining Innovation (SI) is the third type of innovation. SI relies on BR and BI to improve what already exists. This type of innovation starts with a well-defined problem and is most familiar to Leaders across industries. This approach asks, *We have x, now how can we make it better?*

The fourth and final type of innovation is Disruptive Innovation (DI). With DI, Leaders create a culture that says, *I'm going to create x and generate a market for x.* With this type of innovation, the problem is not well defined and the market may not be accessible until after development. Smartphone technology was developed using this type of innovation. Yes, there was a time when we left home without phones and the world did not end. Remember when we went to record stores, combed through racks of albums, purchased multiple albums and painstakingly made mix tapes? Now, we can stream thousands of songs to our smart phones without rolling out of bed?

It is not necessary for Leaders to commit to a single type of innovation. For maximum profitability and growth potential, Leaders should encourage a culture of innovation that utilizes all four types of innovation.

Innovation Manifesto

During a beta test of this book, Leaders told me that just reading about the different types of innovation was overwhelming. The Leaders were still focused on supply and demand. So if you are feeling a little overwhelmed from reading the previous section and thinking to yourself, *I have so many other things I need to prioritize first*, let me challenge you to file the types of innovation away until you get to the end of this book. Don't beat yourself up (don't beat me up, either). Remember, 92% of CEOs from organizations with revenues greater than $1 billion did not prioritize innovation. Now you understand why.

Next, I'm going to introduce my *Innovation Manifesto*. Let's do a learning check. You learned the meaning of key words and four types of innovation. Now, let's address some beliefs.

My manifesto is comprised of seven fundamental beliefs that I believe every Leader must have to create a culture of innovation. Leaders must believe:

I.   Innovation is my legacy.

II.   Couponing is not innovation.

III. Imagination > Memory.

IV. Leaders are not lion tamers.

V.   Leadership capacity determines innovation capacity.

VI. Leadership evolution will set the pace for innovation.

VII. Innovation requires community.

Okay. The foundation is laid. Now, let's stretch you and grow you to develop a mindset that fits a more empowering framework for leading change.

There's still power in writing things down. Fill in the blanks with correct answers from the *Leadership Innovation Manifesto*.

I.   Innovation is my _____.

II.   _____ is not innovation.

III. _____ > _____.

IV. Leaders are not _____ _____.

V.   Leadership _____ determines _____ capacity.

VI. Leadership _____ will set the _____ for innovation.

VII. Innovation requires _____.

Innovation is not optional.

I. INNOVATION IS MY LEGACY

An Ancient King

I WANT TO INTRODUCE you to King Hezekiah. Hezekiah is believed to have reigned as the 12th king of Ancient Judah sometime between 716—687 BC. To put Ancient Judah in context, the modern geographical boundaries are Israel and Palestine. He rose to power during a very challenging time and for all intents and purposes, he was a successful king for that time. Unfortunately, like all heroes, he was flawed and made one egregious mistake.

King Hezekiah is mentioned in Jewish, Christian and Muslim texts as being a true leader of his generation. When you're good at what you do, others become curious about you. It's the same thought pattern behind top influencers following each other on social media and in the industry. Well things were not much different in ancient times. Other kings were curious about King Hezekiah and often asked to meet with him to learn his secrets to success. One king was particularly curious about Hezekiah, this king ruled the kingdom of Babylon. The geographical location of Babylon today is Iraq. Despite being warned not to show all of his treasures to the Babylonian King, pride got the best of King Hezekiah. Hezekiah showed everything. Not a single secret stash was hidden from the Babylonian King's eyes.

When one of Hezekiah's most trusted prophets, Isaiah, learned of Hezekiah's carelessness to say he was upset, fails to do Isaiah's anger enough justice. Isaiah warned Hezekiah that the same king from Babylon would come and take everything in the palace, including Hezekiah's predecessors. This is significant because a monarchy is only as good as the next heir. During Isaiah's lament and warning, Hezekiah quietly thought to himself, "There will be peace and security in my lifetime."

Seems like a harmless thought until you interpret the magnitude of it. As a king who lived through the pain of previous generations failing to leave a healthy legacy, Hezekiah understood the privilege and responsibility of his role in preparing the way for the next generation. But there he was being told the consequences of his actions and taken to task for putting the next generations in danger, only to think to himself, "I'll be dead and gone by the time there are repercussions for it." In other words, *That's the next person's problem.*

A Paradigm Shift

As a doctoral student at University of Miami, an epistemology course was required for graduation. Epistemology is the science of knowledge and how we come to know the difference between truth and opinion. Every field offers an epistemology course at the PhD level. The bible of epistemology courses is Thomas Kuhn's *The Structure of Scientific Revolutions*.

In the book, Kuhn esoterically describes how scientific revolutions are triggered by either an anomaly or crisis. Faced with an anomaly or crisis, a paradigm shift occurs in which old paradigms are replaced with new paradigms. New knowledge is generated from the new paradigms. If I were to describe Kuhn's work in two words, it would be *disruption* and *innovation*.

Current business paradigms are not working. We now live in an era where cash does not change hands. You can buy a house with cryptocurrency, technology is woven into every facet of life, and texting is as natural as talking. A single department can be comprised of 3-4 different generations (Baby Boomers, Gen X, Millennials, and Gen Z) and the COVID-19 pandemic is accelerating shifts in workforce demographics. So why are we using decades old strategies in business today? Stay with me.

A Leadership Revolution

What does an ancient Judean king and a scientist have in common? Both stories demonstrate that nothing happens at random. The warnings or red flags are always present before the event that creates the shift. Depending on who you ask, we are experiencing an anomaly or crisis in every industry. We were warned for decades that the changes we are seeing would come. So if things feel off in your industry, that's why. A common reaction to an anomaly or crisis is seeking alternatives and modifications. In today's current economy we are passed the point of alternatives and modifications. Add a catastrophic event or two and change is no longer optional and slight modifications are insufficient. Change becomes a requirement for organizational survival. We are at the point where entire industries need to be torn down and rebuilt. As such, every industry requires innovative Leaders today more than ever.

I know that's a hard pill to swallow for most Leaders because it:

1. requires change
2. requires learning a new mindset when you may be at the point in your career when you have finally hit a seemingly sustainable stride, and
3. you don't have a map or algorithm to follow.

It's even harder when you introduce inter-generational conflicts within every sphere of the organization. Far too many Leaders are responding like King Hezekiah, *By the time this all hits the fan, I will be retired or moved on.*

For today's Leader, innovation is not optional. Innovation is your responsibility. The speed at which change is happening is not the next person's problem. It's your problem. Therefore, the first belief is, *Innovation is my legacy.* Because even if you're not at the helm of leadership when everything erupts, you will be on the receiving end as the consumer. What do you want to leave behind in your industry?

Mindset Shift Questions

I.   What changes are you seeing in your industry?

_____

_____

_____

2. What kinds of leadership skills are needed for the changes? Do you possess these skills?

_____

_____

_____

3. How can you better equip yourself to lead your organization through the paradigm shifts of your industry?

_____

_____

_____

Cost savings is not an innovative approach.

II. COUPONING IS NOT INNOVATION

Innovation 101

Innovation is a sexy word for the 21st century Leader. *Most Innovative Organization* is a coveted title, yet often undeserving to the majority of organizations. Here's why. Typically, organizations will alter a few processes or approaches, but the majority of outdated operations and culture will remain.

There is power in words. Knowing what words truly mean is one of the secrets of effective influence. Innovation is defined as, *to make an existing thing different.* We can see clear examples of disruptive innovation in the tech industry: Apple, Microsoft, Google and Amazon. An organization with a true culture of innovation strives to change the way things are done permanently in its industry. Remembering life before computers, smartphones and Amazon Marketplace is now a challenge, which was the point.

Innovation in any industry is birthed from the intersection of imagination, talent, human need, and human desire. I'm going to use our smart devices as an example. When you think of our current roster of smart devices, they were a figment of our imaginations in the 1980s. But when imagination meets talent, a spark happens. The technology was developed via Basic Research and Breakthrough Innovation, introduced to the consumer via Disruptive Innovation and today we benefit from Sustained Innovation. The creators of our smart devices leveraged our need for connection and our desire for convenience. Industry Leaders created devices to satisfy that need. If you want to see someone panic, hide their smart device. Our need and desire for the devices are only increasing as the devices become more interconnected with each other and various aspects of daily living. The innovation and advancement of technology is so constant, leasing devices is now more attractive than owning them because who wants to be generations behind in technology. Yet organizations are *behind* every day!

Innovation in the healthcare industry comes from a different source than the tech industry. Innovation in healthcare is typically driven by the need for cost reduction. PR campaigns will say that innovation is driven by the desire for "patient-centered care," but that's only partially true. Society likes to believe that healthcare innovation comes from some intrinsic fountain of good, but the reality is it does not. Vaccines were developed to address public health crises; sickness and death impacting populations is costly. Ultimately, the motivation to drive innovation in healthcare is rooted in industrialized nations' need to extend years of productivity within the population. In the crudest of terms, a healthy population is the key factor in a healthy economy. Healthy economies rely on a healthy and available workforce that can contribute skills and labor continuously. An unhealthy population cannot contribute at the level of productivity needed to thrive economically. In healthcare, change typically does not happen until survival is threatened and change becomes necessary.

Economists have sounded the alarm since the 1960s about the cost of healthcare. President Nixon formally addressed it on July 10, 1969. Fast forward to the 1980s, President Regan sounded the alarm again. In 2009 President Obama talked about the same issue, and in 2018, year 49 of the crisis, President Trump said it again. With all of these warnings, it is understandable why healthcare leaders would cite cost reduction as a top priority. Just about every attempt at innovation in the healthcare industry revolves around the bottom line. And therein lies the problem. When Leaders prioritize cost savings and erroneously see this approach as innovative, no value is added to the organization and it actually hemorrhages human capital.

My Mom's Couponing

As a child, one of my favorite things to do on Saturday mornings was to make a big bowl of cereal and sit in front of the TV. I knew I had from 6:30am until Soul Train aired at 12:00pm to watch whatever I wanted to watch. I somehow understood that six hour window of freedom even before I could officially tell time. I would wake up early and eagerly only on Saturdays, march to the kitchen, take out my bowl, spoon, and milk, and go to the pantry to grab at least one of my three favorite cereals. I always felt loved by my mother. Except when she purchased the store brand of cereal.

"It's the same thing," she would say.

"Lies!" I would scream (In my head, of course. I was disappointed, not crazy).

In my elementary school aged wisdom, the 60 cents savings meant a few key ingredients and I believed a few less food scientists were involved in the design process. Those missing ingredients and a team taking the time to figure out how to ensure that each flake was coated with milk, altered the entire cereal eating experience for me. I was convinced Jesus would not be pleased with my mother's couponing. Dry cereal simply was not of God.

Couponing and Innovation

Innovation is the intersection of imagination, talent, human need and human desire. Not scarcity. Not poverty. Innovation is not cheap. It often requires an upfront investment. Innovation is not safe. It requires risk.

Too many Leaders are couponing and calling it innovation. Save a bit here. Trim here. Learn that practice. Become more efficient. Where is the push to bring in revenue that rewards innovation? Dare I say it, but the organization may need to support the invention of something. There's money in licensing a process, object or service. How will the innovation be sustained? We cut costs and celebrate. We fail to think about how to bring in more money. Notice that I did not write, *save more money*. I wrote, *bring in more money*. My mother may have thought that she was being innovative. Pinching here and there to save on our household budget. While I believe she had the best intentions, she compromised the quality of the experience. Oftentimes, couponing compromises quality because although it saves cost it doesn't always add value.

Ever wonder why organizations seem to have a never-ending stream of quality improvement consultants? The answer that's typically given is, *It's because you're never done with quality improvement*. I should know, I teach QI to doctoral students who are Leaders of healthcare organizations. But anyone who has ever robbed Peter to pay Paul or shuffled money between accounts, knows exactly what's happening. There's a cost to save. Cutting corners here will require you to pay there. Wherever the organization cuts cost results in a sacrifice somewhere else. We are continuously trimming costs and calling it innovation. We are couponing in our own organization and that's not innovation.

Mindset Shift Questions:

1. When you trim costs, what additional revenue could you bring in?

_____

_____

_____

2. What does the organization do well? Could you package it, license it and sell it?

_____

_____

_____

The trap of memory warrants caution.

III. IMAGINATION > MEMORY

Aging and Leadership

Thanks to social media and the tech boom, it can appear as if the Leader of every company is young and sports a hoodie with jeans. The reality is that a young Leader is still a rarity. Trust me. I'm usually the youngest (and most tan) in every c-suite I walk into, if you know what I mean. In a recent study of CEOs, at over six hundred Fortune 500 and S&P 500 companies between 2012 to 2017, the average age of CEOs increased from 45 years old to 50 years. Keep in mind, that's just an average. The raw ages may vary across industries.

The increase in the average age of CEOs may be explained by the Dodd-Frank Act of 2010. After the economic recession in 2008, the Dodd-Frank Act placed greater responsibility on the CEO. This caused boards to want more "seasoned" CEOs at the helm. The problem with the Dodd-Frank Act and aging is that it forces leaders to err on the side of caution due to biological changes in the brain and fear.

Now I'm not rallying to repeal the Dodd-Frank Act, but we need to understand why we may be seeing current patterns in leadership. The key drivers for creating new paradigms and innovation is imagination and creativity. A truly innovative leader must possess the ability to see beyond the organization's current resources while simultaneously meeting the expectations of the Board of Directors, employees, and consumers.

The challenge for most people is that as we age, creativity declines. This decline in imagination and creativity can be influenced by decreases in neural conduction speed, memory, and stamina. Easy...before you go calling me an Ageist, I'm not done. Although there may be neurological changes that explain the decline in imagination and creativity, the single most contributing factor is fear. As we age, we become more reliant on memory. We also have more to lose. Risk takes on a different meaning in our 50s and 60s than it did in our 20s. Memory gives Leaders the luxury of being more confident of predicting an outcome and risk is lowered. Most adults fear failure. They are especially fearful of failing in front of other people.

Andragogy

My last few years in higher education gave me a front row seat to observing this fear in action. In simple terms, andragogy is the study of adult learners. Child development theories do not apply to adult learners. In my field, the average age of a doctoral student is 45 years old. What works for the 18-year-old freshman will not work for the 45-year-old with a 20-year career, a mortgage and dependents. The 18-year-old may not study for the test. The 45-year-old may study too much and launch right into a panic attack. So, what's the difference?

Memory does not work in a doctoral program and adult learners fear failure. It's new territory that requires a different approach to acquiring knowledge. Doctoral study is all about creating new neural pathways. When a student is overly reliant on memory and clear algorithms for outcomes, doctoral study is a struggle. With adult learners the stakes are much higher and there are more people watching. We can apply this same concept to the average CEO.

The fear older adults experience is rooted in the acceptance of the lie that failure should only happen when we're young. Failure has no age limit. Failure is simply a mode of learning. Do you know what failure tells you? *Don't do it that way.* We personify failure and believe that it reflects who we are. If no one has ever told you this before, let me be the first to tell you, *failure is not meant to be a defining moment or concept in anyone's life.* Think about it. If failure was meant to have the actual power that we give it, nothing would get done. Children would never learn any basic life skills (walking, talking, feeding themselves, getting dressed, etc). I love observing children under the age of three years old because they are fearless. So how does the fearless three-year-old become the 60-year-old CEO who can no longer take risks?

The CEO stops imagining. The goal of risk reduction is to reduce the likelihood of unknown outcomes. By relying on memory, Leaders satisfy their own desire for safety. In mitigating risk, leaders suppress innovation within the organization.

Win/Win

But what if Leaders could meet their obligations while embracing innovation? What if Leaders saw this season of their lives as the opportunity to take the biggest risks? I once had a 94-year-old patient who was filled with so much joy. I asked her for her secret to life, and she said,

Baby, I feel like these are the best years of my life. I can do all the dumb stuff I couldn't do when I was younger. I can't get pregnant. My kids are grown so I already know how they turn out. I've been married a few times. I've experienced birth, death, being rich, being poor. At this age, there's nothing left to fear because I've lived through it all and I'm still here. If I had known then what I know now, I would have lived my life less carefully.

Memory was never meant to be a crutch or a safety net. The fundamental purpose of memory is to help us make decisions more efficiently. Familiar neural pathways reduce decision time. Think about your morning routine from the moment your alarm clock goes off to the moment you walk out the door. Do you need to learn how to button your pants or put on your shoes every morning? No. Thanks to memory.

When I was an undergraduate student, I worked as a Research Assistant in a Cognitive Psychology lab. My job was to assist with a memory experiment where two volunteers had to sit in cubicles that prevented them from seeing what was in front of the other person. The objective was to place a series of pictures in the right order. I watched in awe as two complete strangers utilized memory and developed their own language over a series of rounds. In each round I recorded the amount of time it took for them to complete the task. With every team of participants, the task completion time decreased significantly from the first round to the last round.

Now what if instead of harkening back to successful moments in your career and trying to recreate them, you used the memories of those moments to accelerate success? You already know one possible outcome so you're not starting from scratch. Build on top of memory. Instead of starting innovation from Step 1, you can start innovation from Step 342. That's a huge advantage!

Mindset Shift Questions:

1. What was the high point of your career? When did you feel the most innovative and fearless? Recall that moment and write down what made you feel innovative and fearless.

_____

_____

_____

2. Now think about your current organization. What is hindering you from looking like the fearless, innovative version of yourself? What's the worst possible thing that could happen?

_____

_____

_____

3. What's on the other side of the worst possible thing that could happen? Identify three *good* things that

could happen as a result of the "worst possible thing" that could happen.

_____

_____

_____

To hire talent before your organization is ready for it is the greatest tragedy.

IV. LEADERS ARE NOT LION TAMERS

The Lion and the Kitten

I LOVE SOUTH AFRICA. It is truly my second home. Of course, you can't go to South Africa and not see the Big 5 (elephant, Lion, rhinoceros, cape buffalo and leopard). There's something about a Lion that just leaves me dumbfounded. Their strength, power, and confidence are inherent. When a Lion crosses in front of your path, you stop. Period. They truly are a sight to see, especially in their natural habitat. A Lion is more than a big cat. When I hear "big cat" I think of Mr. Snuggles, the obese family house cat. Mr. Snuggles loses to the Lion every time. You take a giant step over Mr. Snuggles.

The Lion

Most job descriptions are written for Lions. The hiring department gets together and tries to capture everything that can possibly be done by a person hired for the desired position. Even if the chances of executing a specific task is less than 1%, they throw it in the job description. Sometimes I wonder if organizations ever really expect someone to do 100% of the job description. Most job descriptions today actually require two or three employees to fulfill the responsibilities listed. When this happens, it's due to:

A. Leaders have been burned by an underqualified hire in the position before and they are being extra cautious;

B. Leaders genuinely do not know what they want;

C. Leaders really don't want to hire someone in the position.

Sometimes, even with all of the uncertainty and indecisiveness from Leaders about a position, you get a Lion applicant. An applicant that fits the job description *and* can give you a little more. You know when a Lion walks in for the interview. Chances are Leaders have already decided that they will hire the Lion and the interview is just to confirm what Leaders believe they already know. Everyone puts on a great show for this candidate. The candidate is interviewed all day. The true sign is the Tour. If the candidate gets the Tour, then an offer is likely. There's excitement throughout the entire organization. Of course, the Lion gets the job.

Lion Tamers

In my experience, organizations love to boast about the talents of their workforce. I typically get called in when there is a problem with turnover or poor employee retention. Instead of boasting about talent I hear,

> *They have no loyalty.*
> *They don't stay past 2 years.*
> *They aren't resilient enough.*
> *They never planned on staying after they completed their degree.*

Most of the comments reflect the personal frustration of the Leaders more than what's going on with the employees.

Now, a part of my due diligence is collecting data directly from the employees too. Perspective is quite a thing. Either the organization is up in flames or doing fine—it just depends on who I'm talking to. No gray area. My role is to find the truth, which is often hidden somewhere in the gray area no one thinks exists because much to both sides' chagrin, problems with an organization's human assets is never attributed to exactly what either side thinks or says.

When I speak to the employees, what do you think I hear? A completely different perspective. I hear,

> *There's no opportunity for growth unless you stay here forever.*
> *I got my degree and there is no position for me.*

The Leadership Innovation Manifesto

When people find out you're too good, you get a giant target on your back.

Leaders hire top talent like Lions, but by the time they leave they are Kittens. Insecure, unsure of their talents and abilities, wounded and no longer ready to conquer. So, what does that tell me? Lions who are not thriving tell me a lot about the culture of the organization. When Lions can't thrive, they resign. High turnover signals an organization that is not ready for high performers and top talent. Most employees who resign leave feeling pretty defeated—a fraction of the person who initially walked through the doors. Here's the thing: They did not underperform. Oftentimes they overperformed and Leaders had a problem with it. Instead of being truly effective Leaders, the Leaders become Lion Tamers.

Have you ever sat and processed what a Lion tamer actually does? Lion tamers use conditioning to train the animal to rely on human approval over instinctual drives (things the animal is born to do) for the safety and entertainment of humans. Lion tamers turn Lions into Kittens. How does a Lion go from being a majestic beast that makes you stop dead in your tracks when you see one in its natural habitat to something you are cheering and clapping for when it gets up on its hind legs on command? You can probably imagine how the Lion feels. Everything about being tamed must feel wrong. To go from being at the top of the food chain in the wild to performing at a fraction of your abilities for treats has to eat away at a Lion's self-esteem. Now imagine how the Lions in your organization feel.

My 1:1 coaching programs are filled with Lions who were transformed into Kittens. How did this happen? They experienced burnout. Imagine knowing that you were created for a specific purpose, spending much of life attaining skills needed to execute that purpose, then having that drive forced out of you systematically?

Dr. Richard Gunderman refers to this phenomenon as *tiny betrayals of purpose*. He originally developed the concept to explain why physicians experience burnout. The World Health Organization defines burnout as a collection of syndromes that include emotional exhaustion, depersonalization or disconnection, and loss of confidence resulting from unmanaged work related stress. Gunderman believed that individuals select medicine as a profession because they want to help people. However, as early as medical school, they soon learn that the business of healthcare controls the art and science of medicine and everyone does not have altruistic motives for joining the profession. An internal struggle ensues when they see a patient mistreated due to regulation, cost containment, error, poor bedside manner, etc and cannot do anything to stop it or undo it. Each occurrence is a tiny betrayal of purpose. Eventually, hundreds to thousands of these tiny betrayals of purpose accumulate and the physician experiences moral distress and burnout.

In my coaching practice, I find that tiny betrayals of purpose are not unique to physicians. High performing individuals in all industries experience tiny betrayals of purpose. I work with Leaders from healthcare, tech, finance, education, information science, design, transportation and more. And I see the same thing. They come to me because they are in burnout and questioning their path. They lose all confidence and forget that they are Lions. Session after session reveal the same thing: an organization with Leaders who were not ready for Lions.

Innovation requires Lions. It requires employees who can work well in teams, are loyal to the organization, legacy minded, relentless, able to identify and pursue opportunities with laser focus. The problem with Lions is that they are a risk for leaders. They are always trying new things, testing boundaries and choosing imagination over memory; all no-no's for leaders who rely on memory over imagination. To prime an organization for innovation, Leaders cannot be Lion tamers.

Mindset Shift Questions:

1. What do you believe is your role in innovation within your organization?

_____

_____

_____

2. Is your team primarily composed of Lions or Kittens?

_____

_____

_____

3. Were they always this way? If not, what changed?

_____

_____

_____

To predict the success of the company, look to the Leaders.

V. LEADERSHIP CAPACITY DETERMINES INNOVATION CAPACITY

Kodak's Story

LET'S LOOK AT the infamous story of Kodak. How did a company go from being the top company for amaeteur photography to being virtually unknown to an entire generation? Let's look at timeline that spans about 100 years. In 1881, a high school dropout and a businessman formed the Eastman Dry Plate Company. In 1888, the first Kodak camera hit the market. In 1896, Kodak sales of cameras reached 100,000 at $5 each. In 1900, the Brownie camera was introduced at $1 per camera. In 1901, the Eastman Dry Plate Company and the Kodak Company merged to form the Eastman Kodak Company. The company became simply known as Kodak. In 1929, Kodak created the first film that can be used for motion pictures with sound and revolutionized the film industry. In 1975, an engineer at Kodak invented the world's first digital camera. In 1980, Kodak entered the clinical imaging and diagnostic market. In 1999, Kodak sold it's digital printer, copier/duplicator and roller assembly operations to Heidelberger Druckmaschinen AG. In 2012, the New York Stock Exchange warned Kodak that it may be delisted and Kodak filed for bankruptcy days later. Still with me?

Kodak's story provides some insight into Leader's ability to hinder innovation. Leaders directly influence the culture of innovation within an organization, hence the purpose of this book. What happened with Kodak did not happen due to lack of talent or resources. Some of the top scientists in the world worked for Kodak. What happened with Kodak was the Leader's capacity for innovation was capped at the traditional camera that utilized film. The CEO simply could not fathom digital cameras.

The Catalyst

My father loved photography. We have photo albums filled with memories captured on film. Kodak was the top company for the film-based business model, a coveted title they held for 98 years. Kodak was also the top company for photography, among amateur and professional photographers alike. The digital camera was invented by a Kodak engineer, Steve Sasson in 1975. What an incredible idea! Filmless photography. Sasson told the New York Times about management's reaction to his invention at the time. He recalled being told, in essence, *That's cute, but don't tell anyone about it.*

Were the Leaders at Kodak horrible people? No. They were simply unable to fathom the disruptive innovation of digital photography. Even in 2007, Kodak's Leaders wanted to remind the world of Kodak's history as the creator of film. Here's where it gets interesting. Despite management's comment about not telling anyone about the technology, the head of market intelligence, Vince Barabba, researched the likelihood of consumers opting for digital cameras over film cameras. Barabba's study was conducted in 1981 after SONY introduced the first electronic camera. The results showed that digital cameras could potentially replace film cameras, however, this would take at least 10 years to occur. Kodak had a 10-year head start! They had the data, the digital camera and almost a century headstart in brand recognition among consumers. Kodak had this, right? Wrong.

Innovating the Wrong Way

Now with this information, we would think that Kodak's Leaders would have instructed engineers to focus on Disruptive Innovation. That's the difficult decision one of the founders (Eastman) made when he transitioned the business from dry plates to film. Kodak has been down this road before. So what happened this time?

This time they focused on Sustaining Innovation. Leaders did not fully grasp the problem and insisted on the wrong approach. Yes it's easy to sit in this century and pass judgement on the Leaders of Kodak at the time, but this was a capacity problem. Not an intelligence problem. The Barabba report outlined the problem, predicted the market impact and assessed all potential challenges. The facts were presented. So what happened? Barabba's report did not assess the *mindset* of the Leaders.

Understanding Capacity

Capacity is the fixed amount an object can hold. With inanimate objects, capacity is a fixed concept. A one-gallon jug can hold no more than one gallon of liquid. A teaspoon can hold just under 5 milliliters of liquid. And so forth. Human beings do not have the same limitations. Our capacity is theoretically limitless. So how are some organizations seemingly stuck while others are forerunners for innovation? An organization's capacity for innovation is directly tied to the Leader's capacity for innovation.

Being the #1 film business for almost a century made the Leaders at Kodak comfortable at a certain capacity that could not bring the organization forward. The truth is, the Leaders were simply not comfortable with taking a risk on a new business model. By limiting their capacity for innovation, the Leaders limited the capacity and subsequent growth of the organization.

Capacity and Leadership

If Leaders are uncomfortable with expanding their capacity, then they will create an environment that stifles innovation. Some do it consciously, but most do it unconsciously.

I believe many Leaders may be unknowingly battling their own burnout. A Leader in burnout is a Leader in survival mode. In this state, Leaders temporarily lose their ability to assess problems, see opportunities, and take risks. Just as certain as water rolls downhill, Leaders in burnout create organizational cultures that stifle innovation and growth. The focus is on simply surviving and not failing publicly. Their capacity is significantly lower.

Leaders at Kodak simply operated at their capacity, I believe that they were not consciously stifling innovation. To expand capacity, a Leader must be in a state of mind where they are comfortable being expanded. They must be willing to be uncomfortable. When engaging in Breakthrough Innovation, no one knows the answers. With Kodak, the problem was clearly defined. From 1981 on, the Leaders of Kodak should have been guided by one question: *Despite improvement in technology, consumers' desire to capture memories will not change. How will Kodak be the #1 business in capturing these moments in the digital age?*

Mindset Shift Questions:

1. How do you feel about your leadership capacity for innovation?

_____

_____

_____

2. Identify one opportunity for innovation where you led the charge?

_____

_____

_____

3. Identify one opportunity for innovation where you challenged or opposed proposed changes?

_____

_____

_____

4. What were the differences between the two opportunities? Why did one make you say *Yes* and the other make you say *No*?

_____

_____

_____

If you see a leader who refuses to evolve, then you see a company that is getting ready to die.

VI. LEADERSHIP EVOLUTION WILL SET THE PACE FOR INNOVATION

An Air Mattress

S AN FRANCISCO, CALIFORNIA is notorious for its cost of living. An email between two roommates struggling to pay rent started off innocently. Who would have thought that a simple hustle to pay rent would disrupt an entire industry?

> *I thought of a way to make a few extra bucks—turning our place into a "designers' bed and breakfast" — offering young designers who come into town a place to crash during the 4-day event, complete with wireless internet, a small desk space, sleeping mat and breakfast each morning.*

The date of the email was September 22, 2007 and it was between Joe Gebbia and Brian Chesky, co-founders of Airbnb. Two men and one woman attending a design conference responded. Each guest paid $80 per night. Gebbia and Chesky even added tour services.

In 4 days, they made about a thousand dollars. Former roommate, Nathan Blecharczyk, joined the party and airbedandbreakfast.com was formed. The 'air' did not mean flight, it meant air mattresses. In December 2007, the alarms started to go off warning economies around the world of a coming recession. In summer 2008, fifteen investors turned the founders of Air Bed and Breakfast down. On September 15, 2008, Lehman Brothers crashed.

Airbnb was founded in 2008 as an online community marketplace where regular people can list and book short-term lodging accommodations in almost 200 countries. In 2008, Hoteliers scoffed at the entire concept of homeowners operating as boutique hotels and offering space to strangers. Today, Airbnb's total number of listings surpasses the top five major hotels combined. How did this happen?

Leadership Evolution

A privilege of being a Leadership Coach is that I get a front row seat to my clients' evolution. There are several things that need to take place in order to evolve from one phase of leadership to the next. Contrary to popular belief and practice, leadership evolution is not measured by titles and promotions. There are plenty of c-suite level executives who have primal approaches to leadership, and this is not the goal. Primal Leaders operate from a place of fear, and poison every relationship they have, professional and personal. In my practice, leadership evolution is measured by how a Leader responds to challenges (and stress) in all areas of their lives. Evolution happens when they can stand firm amid the chaos and learn the lessons needed for the next level of leadership and life.

Evolution requires a Leader to assess all aspects of themselves to determine how to avoid growing in a lopsided way. We all know lopsided leaders. Performance is optimal and they appear to be successful, but their spiritual life is non-existent, intimate relationships are falling apart, two out of three children are in rehab and child number three only communicates when money is needed. Their identity is so wrapped up in a single entity (their position or career) that trying to separate the person from the position usually means one coaching session of just questions and tears. Lopsided evolution is detrimental to a Leader's well-being. This kind of Leader is not ready to evolve nor are they ready to lead innovation.

Innovation requires optimal conditions. Optimal conditions are set by the right combination of stress, a mindset primed for innovation, and a supportive and competent leadership team. If the organization is not striving to be number one in their niche, then why does it exist? A mindset primed for innovation sees obstacles as opportunities and retirement is not the end goal. Industry changing legacy is the end goal. Highly evolved Leaders are sensitive to these conditions and know how to maneuver the organization through them. They know how to catch the current, instead of trying to swim against it. Poorly evolved leaders are sensitive to only a few conditions and become hyperfocused on them—ultimately missing opportunities for innovation.

Evolution and Innovation

The pace at which innovation takes place within an organization is directly tied to the Leaders' evolution. Leaders who have a healthy pace of evolution are agile and adapt efficiently. There is no separation of their professional life from their personal life and they don't wear masks. They seem to be right on target with their industry, anticipate disruption and know how to stay ahead of the curve. These Leaders embrace opportunities for innovation.

Leaders who no longer evolve, will not innovate. They will rely on memory and "tried and true" approaches to current problems. Leaders who evolve at a slow pace will often take delayed action and cause the organization to miss opportunities.

As of the date of publication of this book, Airbnb is just over 10 years old. Hilton Hotel celebrated 100 years of service in 2019. Marriott hotels have been in operation for 92 years, and Westin 89 years. What was so different about the founders of Airbnb? Not that much. Hilton's first hotel was the conversion of his father's general store into a 10-room hotel. Westin started as Western Hotels (then Western International Hotels) and was originally a property management company launched during the Great Depression in 1930. The concept of offering strangers lodging as they passed through town is centuries old. Most of the world knows the story of an innkeeper, a stable, a young couple, a donkey and a manger, so the founders of Airbnb were not introducing a far-fetched concept. They just did it better and faster.

Leaders of major hotel chains took too long to evolve and subsequently missed vital opportunities for innovation. Leaders at Airbnb evolved at a rapid pace, listened attentively to the market and innovated accordingly. Gebbia, Chesky, and Blecharczyk tried to launch Airbnb three different times between 2007 and 2008. With each failed attempt, they re-evaluated, adjusted and re-launched. The market demanded that Leaders in the lodging industry evolve at a rapid pace. Those who didn't were simply left behind. The founders of Airbnb demonstrated an unprecedented level of leadership agility that was not seen in the hospitality industry before. The pace of their evolution was rapid and their organization benefitted quite well from it.

Mindset Shift Questions:

1. Who do you identify with more, the founders of Airbnb or the leaders of the hotel industry? Explain.

    _____

    _____

    _____

2. How would you rate your leadership evolution? Fast, Moderate or Slow? Explain.

    _____

    _____

    _____

3. How would your team rate your leadership evolution?

    _____

    _____

    _____

4. How does your leadership differ from 10 years ago?

_____

_____

_____

5. How does your life differ from 10 years ago?

_____

_____

_____

Team.
Community.

VII. INNOVATION REQUIRES COMMUNITY

Team Building

"**W**HAT'S YOUR RATE for a team building retreat?" asked a booming voice on the other end of the phone.

"I don't offer those as a stand-alone service anymore," I responded.

"But you're a corporate trainer," he retorted.

"I am. But team building exercises are a waste of money in toxic work environments."

I didn't land that contract.

It's no secret that I hate team building retreats. They don't work. Everyone gets together and kumbayas then returns to the Thunderdome known as a department or organization 24 hours later. I've led them and endured them. They are an absolute waste of time and money when they are done in isolation. They are expensive band-aids. It's no different than a couple going on a vacation to "fix" their relationship and as soon as they return home, the arguments restart. In good conscience and as a means of good practice, I just don't offer them anymore as a stand-alone service.

Not Team, Community

A team is a group of people who are working towards a common goal. Sports teams are striving to win championships. Corporate teams strive to meet quarterly and annual goals, but when the goal is removed, what is the purpose of everyone coming together? Leaders need to be clear about this. Once the goals are met, then what? If there is significant change in the team dynamics, then what? Teams rely on star players. Remove the stars and the entire team falls apart. You cannot build a culture of sustainable innovation that way.

I grew up in the suburbs of New York on Long Island. Our house was on a small, triangular shaped street with only ten houses on it. Everyone knew every homeowner and even their extended family. We knew cars, work schedules, even birthdays. We knew each other's cultures too. My house was Little Jamaica. My next-door neighbor was Little Italy. My neighbor across the street was Little Ecuador. The house at the end of the block on the left was Little Guyana. And so forth. It was beautiful.

I remember when I got my first flat tire. I was 18 years old. I was able to make it to my driveway. My next-door neighbor was sitting on his stoop smoking his cigar. His wife would not allow him to smoke his cigars in the house. My neighbor was retired and would spend his mornings having breakfast then going for a walk with his retired buddies on the boardwalk in Long Beach. He returned shortly before I pulled into our driveway and was having his daily smoke. He took one look at my front left tire and started making his way across his lawn.

Now, it should be noted that Long Islanders only walk on grass during an emergency. *Thou shalt not walk on grass on Long Island.* A well-manicured lawn is a source of pride on Long Island, especially among middle-class families. When I got out of the car he asked, "Are you okay?" I had tears in my eyes and was in a panic because I was supposed to pick up my younger sister from school. He knew our schedule and before I could say anything else, he reached into his pocket and pulled out his keys. In his strong New York Italian accent, he said, "Don't worry aboudit [about it]. Here, take my truck and go git [get] your sister. You're home. You're safe." It was one of the kindest gestures someone had ever done for me. He handed a teenager (who was not a blood relative) the keys to his truck. *That* was community.

That's why I encourage Leaders to build community. Community builds beyond the goal. Communities do life together. Members care about each other, they know each other and want to see everyone succeed. Community is the secret to healthy organizational culture and retention. Sustainable innovation requires community. Leaders need people who care beyond the goal, understand each members' strengths and weaknesses, and celebrate milestones of life. Community creates safe space within the organization for highly talented people (Lions) with active imaginations to take risks and evolve.

The most important thing about community is that it builds a culture of trust. Innovation requires risk and a certain level of vulnerability that makes space for failure. Trust creates safe spaces for failure. It also provides fertile ground for success. Some Leaders may scoff at the responsibility of building community and establishing trust, but I assure you, those Leaders are struggling with innovation.

Mindset Shift Questions:

I.   If you were diagnosed with a terminal illness today, which of your coworkers would you tell?

_____

_____

_____

2. Name five of your co-workers.

_____

_____

_____

3. For each co-worker, list at least one major milestone in their life that occurred in the last two years.

_____

_____

_____

4. Think of your best professional experience to date (it does not have to be at your current organization). What made it such a great experience?

_____

_____

_____

LEADERSHIP MINDSETS AND INNOVATION

NNOVATION IS A value-added activity. It is directly tied to growth in every industry and benefits the economy. We know why innovation is important yet struggle with implementation and sustainability. Why?

Because without the right mindset, innovation is a fancy word for change and we naturally focus on the challenges of innovation: risks, resources, and fear of "not getting it right." We forget the Leader's role in driving innovation. The Leaders are the strongest predictor of an organization's capacity for innovation. A Leader can implement all the initiatives, hire the talent, but if the fears mentioned in this book exist and the mindset is not genuinely in favor of innovation, the initiatives will fail. The organization will have a Kodak moment—get it?

Innovation is not just about profit and loss. Business acumen isn't the magic spark that determines if a Leader can create a culture of innovation. Dare I say it, but it may be a stumbling block. Remember the Gartner Report, only 8% of CEOs from companies with revenues over $50 million (most over $1 billion) identified innovation as a priority, yet 53% identified growth as a priority. Now, let's unpack this. If most top execs have an MBA, yet still struggle with identifying innovation as the only thing that adds legacy-level value to an organization, then where is the gap?

The first MBA program was launched at Harvard University Business School in 1908. In my studies of leadership, Maxwell, Nightingale, Carnegie, Bennis, Campbell, Veldsman and the other leadership voices of every generation never talk about profits, percentages, and losses. They talk about people and relationships. Why? Because the key to profits are not found in the bottom line. The profits are found in unlocking the potential of the people within the organization. Creating an environment that uplifts and protects. I know the entire section of your brain filled with indoctrination from your MBA may be tensing up right now, but just stay with me.

MBA programs focus on knowledge and behavior of business, yet neglect vital competencies. The problem with Leaders today is that they have lost sight of the people they are charged to lead within the organization. Decades old management principles (notice I didn't write leadership principles) reflect inherent mistrust of humans. Think about the policies within your own organization. Most of our current management principles favor industrial mindsets. Losing sight of the humanity within the team equates to losing sight of innovation. Too often Leaders do not encourage innovation until it becomes an absolute necessity for survival. Just prior to filing bankruptcy, Kodak's leaders attempted to go after every entity they sold technology to. It was as if they were saying, *Okay, Sasson was a genius. We were wrong to disregard the potential of his invention. You can give it back now.*

A ripe culture of innovation requires Leaders who believe that they have a highly talented workforce and trust them. Innovation and people go hand in hand. Innovation is not always birthed from a formal research program. Silicon Valley leaders are famous for allowing employees to engage in 15—20% of creative time where they are permitted to work on projects unrelated to work.

There are many models about how to implement innovation. These models focus on behaviors. They assume people want the *How* and completely ignore human desire for the *Why*. None of the models mention leadership mindset. Now mindset is not some New Age mumbo jumbo. One of the largest consulting firms in the world specializes in mindset. Mindset is how Leaders see themselves and the world, a filter through which all decisions are made. Conflict arises within organizations because everyone has a different mindset.

When the leadership team has different mindsets for innovation, how can they make hiring decisions that will facilitate the creation of a cohesive innovative culture? I've sat on leadership teams where I was the only member that wanted innovation. It was exhausting. I could see opportunities to grow and move the organization forward. Simple changes that could catapult our national ranking. Leaders would politely listen, then respond with "That's cute," and never tell anybody. To say I grew frustrated is putting it mildly. Amid one moment of frustration, I asked the top two leaders in my college why I was hired. They responded, "To be innovative." I asked the top two leaders in my department with whom I have the most daily contact, why I was hired. They cited all of my talents *except* innovation. I stepped down from that position. It became clear to me that senior leaders wanted innovation and mid-level leaders wanted a work-horse, a place filler. Misaligned mindsets among leadership levels is quite common in organizations and can sabotage innovation.

The greatest predictor of the success of a leadership development program is whether the first thing assessed is the organization's greatest asset and liability, the Leader. Many Leaders have a survival mindset. Leaders with a survival mindset are focused on playing their part to ensure that basic organizational goals are met, usually to keep their job. These are the Leaders who set performance objectives and implement a suite of change initiatives. In contrast, Leaders with a community mindset care about the collective well-being and contribution of all members of the organization. Leaders with a community mindset also have a mindset for innovation. These Leaders are more likely to spend time learning about why the performance trends are occurring before launching into action. In other words, they are likely to take Einstein's advice, *If I had an hour to solve a problem, I'd spend 55 minutes thinking about the problem and 5 minutes thinking about solutions.* As Leaders, it is important that we assess our feelings and beliefs about innovation because the organization's response to innovation will mirror the Leader's response.

CONCLUSION

I'S BEEN A pleasure to come alongside you in the pages of this book. As a Leader, I understand the challenges of innovation. I learned that before I call the consultants and implement strategies, I needed to remove barriers to innovation in my mind first. Everything starts in the mind. A single thought can alter the trajectory of every experience.

My goal for this book is to encourage mindset shifts that will lead to identifying and implementing breakthrough strategies for innovation within your organization. I believe in starting with the leaders and benefiting from the mirroring effect. An organization will always reflect the Leaders. Leaders who truly value innovation and operate from a legacy mindset can build culture of innovation. Leaders who do not, stifle innovation and tame Lions.

At the end of my coaching sessions, I always ask clients to share the greatest revelation they received. I would love to do the same with you.

What's been the most helpful for you from the Leadership Innovation Manifesto? What is one powerful action you will take as a result of reading this book? I want to hear your answer. Head on over to Twitter and tell me (@DrKimHires). I read every tweet.

Visit www.drkimhires.com for additional leader development resources. You can also subscribe to The Leadership Antidote Podcast hosted by yours truly.

COACHING GUIDE

AS I MENTIONED in the beginning, this book can be read as a solo endeavor or as a community building activity for Leaders. To facilitate the group discussions, all discussion questions used in this book are listed below.

1. What changes are you seeing in your industry?

    _____

    _____

    _____

2. What kinds of leadership skills are needed for the changes? Do you possess these skills? If not, how can you acquire the needed skills?

    _____

    _____

    _____

3. How can you better equip myself to lead your organization through the paradigm shifts of your industry?

_____

_____

_____

4. When you trim costs, what additional revenue can you bring in?

_____

_____

_____

5. What does the organization do well? Can you package it, license it and sell it?

_____

_____

_____

6. What was the highpoint of your career? When did you feel the most innovative and fearless? Recall that

moment and write down what made you feel innovative and fearless.

_____

_____

_____

7. Now think about you current organization. What is hindering you from looking like the fearless, innovative version of yourself? What's the worst possible thing that could happen?

_____

_____

_____

8. What's on the other side of the worst possible thing that could happen? Identify three *good* things that could come from the "worst possible thing" happening.

_____

_____

_____

9. What do you believe is your role in innovation within my organization?

_____

_____

_____

10. Is your team primarily composed of Lions or Kittens?

_____

_____

_____

11. Were they always this way? If not, what changed?

_____

_____

_____

12. How do you feel about your leadership capacity for innovation?

_____

_____

_____

13. Identify one opportunity for innovation where you led the charge?

_____

_____

_____

14. Identify one opportunity for innovation where you challenged or opposed proposed changes?

_____

_____

_____

15. What were the differences between the two opportunities? Why did one make you say *Yes* and the other make you say *No*?

_____

_____

_____

16. Who do you identify with more, the founders of Airbnb or the leaders of the hotel industry? Explain.

_____

_____

_____

17. How would you rate your leadership evolution? Fast, Moderate or Slow?

_____

_____

_____

18. How would your team rate your leadership evolution?

_____

_____

_____

19. How does your leadership differ from 10 years ago?

_____

_____

_____

20. How does your life differ from 10 years ago?

_____

_____

_____

21. If your were diagnosed with a terminal illness today, which of your coworkers would you tell?

_____

_____

_____

22. Name five of your co-workers.

_____

_____

_____

23. For each co-worker, list at least one major milestone that occurred in their life in the last two years.

_____

_____

_____

24. Think of your best professional experience to date (it does not have to be at my current organization). What made it such a great experience?

_____

_____

_____

These are powerful questions that require authentic communication in a safe setting. If your organization wants help facilitating this discussion reach out to Dr. Kim at info@drkimhires.com

NOTES

Introduction: Let's Talk About Meaning

1. Jay Fraser, "Etymology of Innovation," https://www.innovationexcellence.com/blog/2014/04/29/etymology-of-in- novation/
2. 'Manifesto' Merriam-Webster Dictionary

The Value of Innovation

1. Thorndike, *The Outsiders: 8 Unconventional CEOs and Their Radically Rational Blueprint for Success.* Published by Harvard Business Review.
2. Gartner 2019 CEO and Senior Business Executive Survey
3. Satell, G. (2013). Before you innovate, ask the right questions. *Harvard Business Review* https://hbr.org/2013/02/before-you-innovate-ask-the-ri
4. Satell, G. (2015). Innovation is the only true way to create value. *Forbes* https://www.forbes.com/sites/

gregsatell/2015/11/29/innovation-is-the-only-true-way-to-create-value/#777199ce18e3

I. Innovation is My Legacy

1. Jacob Issac, "King Hezekiah" an electronic publication of the Kehot Publica- tion Society https://www.chabad.org/library/article_cdo/aid/464023/jewish/King-Heze- kiah.htm
2. Chronicles 32:1-33 NIV
3. Isaiah 39:8 NIV
4. Thomas Kuhn, *The Structure of Scientific Revolutions.*

II. Couponing is Not Innovation

1. Definition of "Innovation" provided by Merriam-Webster online dictionary.
2. "Half A Century Of The Health Care Crisis (And Still Going Strong), " Health Affairs Blog, September 12, 2018. DOI: 10.1377/hblog20180904.457305

III. Imagination > Memory

1. Oliver Staley, "How the average age of CEOs and CFOs has changed since 2012" in Quartz https://

qz.com/1074326/how-the-average-age-of-   ceos-and-cfos-has-changed-since-2012/

2. Dodd-Frank Wall Street Reform and Consumer Protection Act, Pub. L. No. 111-203, § 929-Z, 124 Stat. 1376, 1871 (2010) (codified at 15 U.S.C.

3. Seligman, M.E.P., Forgeard, M., & Kaufman, S.B. (2016). Creativity and aging: What we can make with what we have left. In Seligman, M.E.P., Railton, P, Baumeister, R.F., & Sripada, C. (Eds.), Homo Pro- spectus. New York, NY: Oxford University Press.

IV. Leaders Not Lion Tamers

1. Definition of "Capacity" provided by Merriam-Webster online dictionary.

2. Gunderman, R. (Feb 21, 2014). For the young doctor about to burnout. The Atlantic

3. World Health Organization. Burn-out an "occupational phenomenon": International Classification of Diseases

4. Maslach, C. & Leiter, M.P. (2016). Understanding the burnout experience: Recent research and its implications for psychiatry. World Psychiatry, 15(2), 103-111.

V. Leadership Capacity Determines Innovation Capacity

1. Reuters Business News (Jan 19, 2012). Timeline: The Kodak moment fades.
2. Mui, Chunka (2012). How Kodak Failed in Forbes Magazine.
3. Gann, D. (2016). Kodak invented the digital camera—then killed it.

    Why innovation often fails. World Economic Forum. https://www.weforum.org/agenda/2016/06/leading-innovation-through-the-chicanes/

VI. Leadership Evolution Will Set the Pace for Innovation

1. Daniel Gerdeman/HBS Working Knowledge (2018). The Airbnb Effect: Cheaper Rooms For Travelers, Less Revenue For Hotels. Forbes.
2. Biz Carson and Rebecca Aydin (2019). How 3 guys turned renting air mattresses in their apartment into a $31 billion company, Airbnb. Business Insider
3. Hotels by Golly published in Time Magazine (July 19, 1963).
4. Westin Hotels and Resorts Worldwide—Company Profile, Information, Business Description, History, Background Information on Westin Hotels and Resorts

Worldwide   https://www.referenceforbusiness.com/ his-   tory2/42/Westin-Hotels-and-Resorts-Worldwide. html#ixzz61WzEN4vx

5.   TED Talk 2016. Joe Gebbia: How Airbnb designs for trust

Leadership Mindsets and Innovation

1.   Arbinger Mindset Institute https://arbinger.com/
2.   President & Fellows of Harvard College, "Harvard Business

   School: Key Dates & History," https://www.hbs.edu/ about/facts-and-figures/Pages/his- tory.aspx

D R. KIM HIRES is known internationally for her work on burnout, leadership, and education. She is a Leadership Burnout Coach, Speaker, Author, and host of the Leadership Antidote Podcast. She combines lessons from her career with formal training to help Leaders at all levels develop the mindset and skills needed to become industry Leaders of today and tomorrow. Dr. Kim founded The Nightingale Firm in 2014 after surviving burnout and recognizing that Leaders are seldom trained on how to ensure their well-being. She is on a mission to help every organization in the world become burnout proof safe spaces where everyone can thrive. As Kimberly A. Hires, PhD, RN, her professional career includes degrees and experiences from some of the top institutions in the US including Johns Hopkins University, the National Institutes of Health, and the University of Miami all before the age of 30! She is an award-winning professor and leader development expert. She is wife to an incredible chef and mommy to the most amazing child on the planet. She and her tribe reside in Atlanta, Georgia (USA).

Social Media

Follow Dr. Kim for the latest news, updates and daily inspirations.

    Instagram: @drkimhires
    Twitter: @DrKimHires
    LinkedIn: @Dr. Kim Hires
    TikTok: @drkimhires